COVE

ALSO BY JAMES BRASFIELD

POETRY

Infinite Altars

Ledger of Crossroads

Inheritance and Other Poems (chapbook)

TRANSLATION

The Selected Poems of Oleh Lysheha

COVE

POEMS | JAMES BRASFIELD

LOUISIANA STATE UNIVERSITY PRESS
BATON ROUGE

Published by Louisiana State University Press
lsupress.org

LSU Press Paperback Original

DESIGNER: Barbara Neely Bourgoyne
TYPEFACE: Whitman

Cover photograph: *IRELAND, Connacht, Aran Islands, 1977,* copyright Josef Koudelka / Magnum Photos.

Grateful acknowledgment is made to the editors of the following publications, in which many of
these poems first appeared: *Chicago Review, DMQ Review, Heliotrope, Lincoln Review, Literary Matters,
New Virginia Review, On the Seawall, Pittsburgh Quarterly, Poem-a-Day* (Poets.org), *Poetry Wales, Reed
Magazine, Southern Review, Spire, Stand,* and *Tar River Poetry.* "Place and Time" first appeared in the
essay "Controlling Tone through Syntax," by Robin Becker, *Poetry Newsletter,* September 1, 2019.
"Palladium" was scored by Edward Jacobs for soprano and piano, and premiered in Greenville,
North Carolina, at the *North Carolina NewMusic Initiative,* January 26, 2017.

Note: "Piero: *The Resurrection* of 1467": Lines 15–16, Hemingway, *The Sun Also Rises.*

LIBRARY OF CONGRESS CATALOGING-IN-PUBLICATION DATA
Names: Brasfield, James, author.
Title: Cove : poems / James Brasfield.
Description: Baton Rouge : Louisiana State University Press, [2023]
Identifiers: LCCN 2022036889 (print) | LCCN 2022036890 (ebook) |
    ISBN 978-0-8071-7660-3 (paperback) | ISBN 978-0-8071-7982-6 (pdf) |
    ISBN 978-0-8071-7981-9 (epub)
Subjects: LCGFT: Poetry.
Classification: LCC PS3552.R32755 C68 2023 (print) | LCC PS3552.R32755
    (ebook) | DDC 811/.54—dc23/eng/20220804
LC record available at https://lccn.loc.gov/2022036889
LC ebook record available at https://lccn.loc.gov/2022036890

for Charlotte

The cords of all link back, strandentwining cable of all flesh.

—JAMES JOYCE, *ULYSSES*

CONTENTS

PART I

∎

PALLADIUM

A cortege of clouds'
shifting planes

reflected on a river,
the current's weave deepens,

yet motionless
the dramatization of

a fern unfolding,
light illuminating the air

for a moment's threshold,
when time, where we stand,

corresponds to the day
held firm,

derived from the elegance of
the equation

for what was once never here.

PIERO AND THE SPIDER

(Piero della Francesca)

1.

Window, piazza, cobbles,
fountain and the ripple unbreaking,
brush in hand unfolding oils, tempera on panel,
or pigment to wet walls . . .

distinctions in touch with detachment,
light to each part,
lucent—and he is fastened
to what is changing

and time's affliction lessened,
dab by dab, the brush-point toward
a geometer's summation,
mindful our angles of vision.

Each gesture shapes—
in the pure solitude of an instance,
the silence irenic in Piero's sight—vernacular
passages of color on rectangle, square, or circle,

etcetera the shapes, plane by plane,
variety unvarying
naturally as sprout to sapling,
tree to stone, as on a path dividing the forest

here before the tilled fields,
a path rising,
stretching into the distance,
narrowing at a large, sun-dappled stone in shade—

such weight of presence—
a juncture, virtue of measure,
brushstroke at the farthest point
in the passing light.

2.

A spider in
        the understory,
                a thread from hunger,
branch to branch the impulsion,
a working out of space—

the scripted veil
is woven, ancient the manifestation
of a spider's eyes and spinnerets.

All depends on what by chance
comes to it as if
it were not seen—

an idea drawn from sinews of light
grown splayed against the air,
spit-latched,

an aperture to frame the path,
a seeming transparency,
depth luring a way forward.

3.

The spider waits
diminished, unknowing,
in its three dimensions,
for the illusion to take hold—

its web real, and the moment is
if close enough,
nature's shape, branch to twig,
distilled from compulsion,

and complicated
the violence of the web,
and, caught in Piero's blent
pigments, complex the grace,

its origins unseen
in the patron's commission,
Piero's childhood
baptizing the present,

as when a flock
of doves calling from their arc
of flight—wings
transfixed by sunlight

over the narrow creek—
perched in the olive grove
and became
the luminous dove, open-winged,

suspended under dark leaves crowning
the pale trunk
of a walnut tree—the dove
unreflected on the still water.

4.

Blind, the aged Piero

remembered again perhaps

his translations of light, as if
Plato had been

a fisherman sewing his net

for the deep gold and vermilion
spots of a Tiber trout

and caught it, held it up

in late afternoon's cool light,

seen
to sense life.

MATTER OF LIGHT

A matter of light,
part of the tree's shade over the yard,
a zelkova leaf, narrow palm
of the rust belt in April, green tints,

then little by little turning red,
a leaf surviving first snows, becoming
half furled, wing ruffled,
in the uncharted scales of ice,
their lunar tarnish,

and around it, leaf by leaf departing,
it fashioned a trace of shadow on the ground,
like some thin stripe across a wren's skull
rooted in stillness, bleached in a field,

in January, a warm spell sustaining
last year's leaf. It became in wind
a hand again, frost-burnt but waving
under the slow passing arc of sky,
the leaf tree-loyal
when buds reappeared.

LATE SUMMER

Now cosmos in bloom and snow-in-summer
opening along the garden's stone borders,

a moment toward a little good fortune,
water from the watering can,

to blossom, so natural, it seems, and still
the oldest blooms outside my door are flourishing

according to their seedtime.
They have lived as in trust

of tended ground, not of many seasons
as the lingering bud in late summer,

when leaves have reached their greenest,
when a chill enters the nights,

when a star I've turned to, night after night,
vanished in the shift of constellations.

But when on a bare branch,
even in August, a sprig starts,

sprig to stem—as if to say, See,
there's kinship with the perennials

you think so hardy—voice
the moment among the oaks, toast

the spring in summer, as once each May
a shot of vodka is poured on bare dirt

among gravestones to quench the dead,
among the first stars of this new evening.

ETRUSCANS AT MONTERCHI

After centuries, still the sifting
of afternoon, the homing swallows
circling, shape-shifting,
immersed in what they sense,

and still this moment,
my shadow on the ground, I'm watching
what has never changed,
what seem random curves of flight,

yet their fixed points we'll never see
above the olive grove, each skull aloft
ever since swallows first
emerged in Tuscany, and nearly always

there has been a moment waiting:
its creature watching shadows rise
from earth—and around me
crickets begin their chants overlapping.

FINDING WANG WEI

A red-winged blackbird on the bridge rail
flies, its epaulets brightening the crown of a tall oak,

and sunlight pale through the dark shallows
at the shore, constant the slow, wavering current.

I wait for an orange stone to come
clear through the circulation of silt,

the oval stone arriving like a blood moon
rising through clouds, and I recalling

a barn burning through late winter rain
at dusk, each flame its mute pulse

growing and all time gathered now
in the orange stone as I stare.

■

Bird, oak, stone in March, icy creek
flowing over layers of October leaves

into the lake are textures on Wang's silk scroll,
felt as seen. —He *is* his seeing shared:

I breathe the vision I feel, his mind's translation
to ink brush from emptiness,

from time to place, his patient velocity, and not
that Wang imagines my face when I'm gone.

Come June, I'll lean in closer to Wang's dried scroll
and gaze a long while, turning up my collar

against a March wind, and cross my arms,
feeling their sudden warmth.

THEN RAIN

At the narrow stretch of lakeshore,
dense scrub, thorn and bramble thickets
circle a small pond,

autumn staining the brushwood
shadowing a birch sapling's pale leaves
at this chanced hour,

a warm dusk and stillness over
the pond's still water,
and the birch a Buddha, radiant—

branches akimbo,
reflecting the end of day
in this reprieve from the ends of air:

the dry leaves' rustling stopped,
as never to let go on a day
of second summer

happening within them. Wind
returns to the far shore of the lake,
the current rising,

wavery, lapping the narrow margin of shore
under blackening clouds,
their shapes of mountains

abiding. Deep woods
once unmoving . . .
whitecaps merge with the dark.

DREAM, THE HARNESS

It sat waiting like a farm tool
a long time in the ground.

Weeds grew through its spaces
and high grass
half hid the empty hinges.

The great stillness of its being there
I recognized
was for wings,

though I have never seen
anything like it,

not of angels, nor of steel,
not the light wood for modeled wings, but for
the breadth of a condor's,

left there, lowered from my shoulders.

STONE VALLEY

Sunlight broken on the forest floor,
and the clear creek thawed, winding deep
through a wooded ravine . . . I'm drawn
through second and third growth,

my climb steady, my chest parallel
to the ground. Over twigs snapping
and leaves like primordial things
abandoned by the surf,

I find a branch, bark stripped . . .
nesting crow? . . . the fate of a body's
the fate of a stick.
It breaks under my weight.

What's left holds up, becomes
nearly part of me. Soon,
I can't remember
when or where I found it.

All I see on this angled ground rests
in lengthening shadows. I find a stone,
its jut of clamshell:
minuscule its ridge and trough of ribs.

At the summit, as at a sea cliff,
how strange another night is
moving across what distance in time—
night's darkening tide

over the Appalachians,
having come in at Penobscot, via
the Apennines, risen from a Roman ditch,
Ovid's at the Black Sea,

body to bone, hill to reef.

ROUGH WEATHER

Moths, flickering from the dark,
knock the porch screen, as if
mistaking me for lamplight.
Phosphorescence rekindled,
waves narrow the beach, waves from as far
as I can see—the red pulse of a buoy.

I close my eyes to the wind,
to the surf's release, a relief as from
a dream I came to as a child:

> *a knot tight at its center,*
> *a gray, level thread grew to string, to rope,*
> *the immense knot cropped by the borders of dream.*
> *I tried to wake, to look away,*
> *the rope becoming string, then thread again—*
> *the small knot growing closer . . .*

I open my eyes. The ocean's fury
borne by distance breaks higher
on shore, returning
                              the shadowless afternoon

> I dove into a storm tide
> and swam beyond a drop-off,
> then turned to ride a wave, and folded in the crest,
> my shoulders forced against my face,
> my hands forced
> against my shoulders shoved to the ribbed floor.
> In that roiling time, I felt calm—an autumn bee
> hovering in a jar falling from a table, then
> the bee tapping a closed window above the shards—
> then I was standing, hearing still
> the turbulence that filled the wave,
> its backwash pulling round my legs . . .

Out there, rain comes on.
With its rasping engine, a trawler passes.
Its blinking light grows dim,
hours now before the natural light of dawn.

THE BLUE CEILING

there the points of compass held
—THOREAU

The tide rising—tossing out, taking in—
the spindrift silvered and twilight brightened,
revealing miles traveled by waves.
Over the dunes
a sudden star fell, a sewing needle's flash
through a remnant of dream. All the while
the moon faded to the pale shade of meerschaum
lining my dead father's pipe,
a comfort of gray smoke unspooling
from charred layers, a compulsion
I keep to conjure
him I have no memory of.

Where I slept as a child in the shingled cottage,
my little boy slept at daybreak,
his yesterday inhabiting his dream:
pieces of a puzzle from midday darkening,
then rain, rainbow, then rain,
the summer wind cold, then waves
pounding the beach through night again
below the blue ceiling,
pine knots shining through paint
in lamplight, a room upon pilings
to weather a storm,
as if citadels were possible.

A man now, my son has set compass
to magnetic north of his imagination,
his geometries found for light falling—
line and plane, color and volume—
for light coming back through surfaces:
depths' layered tints a revelation
stilled, constant the radiance forged . . .

A mockingbird began its songs,
trying in succession to choose a song sown
for the moment, as if morning might pass farther away,
and flew, gray wings over a burgeoning surf
then dark sand, and from a dune's brambles
sang, as though at noon a cardinal's cheerful song.

      I hear it nearly a thousand miles away,
      harboring my first days
      there, and return with my son,
      days not to be only
      what they were then, or then . . .

Late that morning we found a whelk,
sea-bleached, its creature absent,
its scoop of mud and broken shells,
its spire begun with a speck of sand,
the work we marveled at,
passing the shell back and forth between us.

PART II

∎

PLACE AND TIME

What you see, have seen,
what you've come to know in accord with place,

what you see at a moment's summation
and in moments of slow understanding,

what was revealed, as you imagined it,
real as you perceived it,

the unfolding verisimilitude
of an absolute evolving through its changes,

like a stone (its shape and color),
when you reached down and saved it—

years later, tossing it away,
not remembering where you found it—

it remains.

AMALGAM

I found the small rock
gleaming with its sparkle of mica
and grains of sand in shadowed
crevices at low tide, an amalgam
from the once alive,
so light it might have flown,

a brain aloft in a seabird's skull,
or wingless it flew, a meteorite shorn
from a distant place, and plunged
as cormorant into the cove's gray water,
a bird searching for a fish
to bring glittering to the surface,

its cosmic weight its own,
fed before it was found, this
rock a remnant, little moon
of our solar system,
I turn in my damp hand
in dry daylight.

PAST CARS SPEED FAST

It is long past, now, long past
and dusk there beginning to fall,
a distant car changing lanes
at something on the road.

I veer to the passing lane—
the dark hazard fast becoming
the deer having stepped
from the forest's edge . . .

All is passing fast—
my car, its vibrations
and sound of wind on the road
closing in on the deer

stretching, twisting her head
to leap out of the way,
and stock-still the body not rising,
and she born in deep woods,

head free from the womb, hooves
together, as if diving, placenta
to existence, her long back legs
immobile till her life landed,

her neck raised from the shadowed floor,
round her the scent of the fresh world,
she now on a swath of four lanes,
fleeing that part of her a corpse already . . .

From insect-spattered windshield
to rearview mirror, the deer a vision:
always the what-has-happened
unfolding from the future, as I speed past.

WANDERERS

A creek flows under the frozen lake.
Canada geese forage a thawed inlet
at the far shore, and from freight of snow
limbs are down and trees, their sapwood rings
and heartwood halted. What it was
in summer leaf-shadow . . .
an owl's clear song, a sparrow flits
thicket to thicket.
Silences are never the same.

In trail ruts rain made, stiff grass
props panes of ice.
Their dark eddies, stilled,
break beneath my boots.
I look back for who I was, years ago.
By now that man has come
to his mother's death—that stillness.
Her touch, her face, her voice
begin their disappearances.
The mystery of death will end,
and he will stand close to who he is
as I've walked down and he to here,
the way by then so disparate.

Turning ahead, I look for him
who led me here, his shoulders hunched
forward. Where I will gain myself descending,
that man ahead, having stood where I am,
is colder among the hemlocks.
This sunlit stone, perhaps, I'll take to him,
this stone perhaps he thought to keep,
put back by the trail. Too far ahead
for him to recall, where he is
is without *this* particular of place.

Our shadow on the shore,
we hear wings plashing from inlets,
geese squawking. They rise, their deep notes
lessen into dusk, the lake
a silver gray, glistening—then, a few
birds chirp, then silence.

PIERO: *THE RESURRECTION* OF 1467

After the long night, a god's pale body
halves the low hills in steepened perspective:
leafless, bleached trees on bare ground—
then, summer trees descending

a burgeoning valley, a village there, perhaps
the painter's, and three tall evergreens rise
above the valley's hill to flat clouds
dark in brightening blue of sunrise . . .

This lean, muscular farmer,
with his scruff of beard, this god aware,
waits to hoist himself, to step forth from limbo
with the calmness of twilight

and of his eyes. Awake in dead stare—
the unbroken pause—his eyes do not see ours.
There's nothing on earth
he would not look at like this.

He's gathered up in his left hand
his coral shroud, his wrist resting on his knee,
his left foot poised on the crypt's high edge—
in his right hand, the gray banner,

its red cross, the triumph over death.
Four soldiers, their shadows cast,
sleep beneath him: the second,
the helmetless one,

a self-portrait—head back against
the banner's staff—dreams what we see . . .
a spider-work of lines on his smock, like veins
their circulation of the risen god . . .

and third—in brass, oval helmet—
leaning on a tilted pike, its blade
at the crown of a summer tree,
at the plane of the god's halo.

For divine favor, stigmata punctuate
the tableau's geometry . . . an endeavor
for city hall and three years' labor
for the god reborn, an awakening

for the painter unto himself unto
the world—this mural,
an ikon's light from within,
anticipating always, now,

last songs of the nightingale
or rooster's first crow
from *this* unending silence
from this victory over death.

TYSMENYTSIA

I. REPRIEVE

(for Lilia Lysheha)

1. *Vigil*

Word has come that my friend is well.
Doctors have carved away the cancer
and, cared for by her brother,
Lilia is home again in Tysmenytsia.
At my window, I'm looking for
a rosefinch flying to an alder
on the banks of the Strýmba
flowing in front of Lilia's house.
What I see in mid-March
is the zelkova, a bonsai subject in Japan,
a tree fast growing, tolerant
of acid rain and the Dutch elm disease
that took the American elm on the berm
where the zelkova's buds are fattening,
as I imagine the buds fattening
in the Carpathian foothills, as all
deciduous trees out in the Alleghenies.
After such vigil, I felt a sad release
when the brown-spotted leaf let go.
It was at first a simple emblem
of endurance. When I heard
of Lilia's illness, the leaf became
a way of thinking of her holding on,
of the possibility of seeing Lilia again,
no matter how far to Ukraine.

2. Winter Precipice

No sound beyond the window—
the leaf's dry tip curled to a beak,
the leaf back a bird's breast
nearly white, the leaf nearly lost
on a night of late snow, the dark

radiance of uncalendared now,
unlike the red, minute hand circling
the green luminous numbers on my black clock
(each day as time held fast), a frost-burnt leaf
an aberration of endurance,

or indifference, isolated in air,
level once with small birds perched
and their whisperings
cast, the leaf spun in wind
through mountain currents of snow.

How, I wondered, did the leaf
maintain its hold to branch,
or branch its catch of stem, or both,
as someone over a precipice
shares a grip of hands.

3. Sphere

Last winter, I walked to the window,
expecting the leaf gone in a moment
of thaw under a blue sky darkening,
and word of snow on the way . . .
gray clouds moving under clouds,
then the burden of snow sticking fast
to the leaf's silhouette of a leaf
hanging on, a parched suspension
at spring's arid border.

On each day of wind
I said through the windowpane,
"Hang on," to the leaf. I wanted
to take a picture, not trusting words
to meld the facets of seeing. I wanted
to make understanding a circumference,
a human way of seeing into.

Had I been a bird on the branch,
I would have heard the leaf ensphered by air,
ever a moment of impulse
quick as a house finch flying from the zelkova,
becoming a rosefinch flying to an alder
leafless along the narrow Strýmba
miles below the Carpathians at dusk.

Now, mid-March,
I hold the leaf, its autumn hue.
A caterpillar has spun filaments
from tip to stem-end, drawing together,
shroud-like, the sides of the leaf,

its ribs sculpting its dry, saw-toothed edges,
its smell of a sweater folded in a drawer
until autumn, a leaf so light,
just breathing blows the leaf across my desk.

4. Days

We turn to the sun rising
and call it morning;

at night we turn away,
as our lives turn
always from us,

and if each tree knew
it shared
a duration such as ours,
what sad forests
we would walk through,

its deep shade like a family tree
from an acorn
from a distant country
from which we sprang,

each of us turning
irreplaceable in the forest,
with life's visitation over,

its glad moments of reprieve.

5. Black Wings

The last time I saw Lilia
was a week in April, in Tysmenytsia—
thaw and rain, bare ground,
leaves sprouting from the alders
along the Strýmba. In Lilia's garden,
daffodils, tiger lilies, roses bloomed,
and the poppies rich in depths of red
as the zelkova in autumn,
but brighter at their height.

White with black markings,
red wattle, comb, and mask,
a rooster on the garden fence
sounded the day and Lilia mixing dough,
rolling it out for varenyky with rose petals:
white tips pinched from stem-ends,
petals mashed with sugar and lemon in a bowl,
folded into pastries and baked—
light the crust, sweet the taste.

All day, Lilia's cats leapt in and out
an open window. A gray cat napped
on a kitchen shelf and a sick rabbit slept
on a towel on the floor, her hurt hen
roosting in a low, open box, chicks
warm under black wings—set free,
the chicks ran wobbling, careening
till she raised her wings:
the chicks rushed back.

In near dark, first the chills, then,
sweat soaked, the fever began,
and across the room the stillness of air

at the window, as I lay on a bed,
and Lilia placed a damp cloth
on my brow. Moonlight moved
slowly to the white wall at the foot of the bed,
where Lilia stood—a shadow
standing watch—till I fell to sleep. . . .

At the garden gate, Lilia
said she was afraid that I would not
return, and I have not—nonetheless,
how close she is, up from the Strýmba.

II. CARPATHIANS

(I. M. Oleh Lysheha)

1. *The Ceramicists*

(above Kosiv, with O.L.)

They were makers of birds, each shape hollow,
clay from their yard, a lung for a whistle,
a compact shrine, its realm of sounds
brought to light as a nightingale's song
is known: each bird its subtle version
as each trusts its altitudes, its nest
made from what's close by . . .

Morning with the makers—trailless,
we climbed green hills into the mountains
as if at each step the mountains were born.

It was afternoon by the time we stopped
to rest in a beech grove. Each of us
pulled leaves from the branches, each leaf
its lemony taste, the leaves' sunlight inside us.

Then, steadily, we formed our column . . .
the terrain steepening, going up a long way—
behind us the sun-dappled ground
again under the trees.

Out from the forest, at a ridgetop,
we stood together on a grassy slope,
the clouds' shadows shifting above
far-off villages and roads
and fields falling away into dusk.

Then we sat
and they began talking
and from their breaths,
from their gentle Ukrainian,
I listened to their music.

2. Apples and the Day

Those who have laid up no store, who live on recognized food,
who have perceived void and unconditional freedom, their path
is difficult to understand, like that of birds in the air.

—THE DHAMMAPADA

Past Rex's house, its rusted roof,
his collar hanging over his door
(long since Rex ran off),
past the neighbors' goat tied
with her kid to their door,
past the horse-plowed field
where a stork broods in the high nest,
Oleh rambles eastward
out of town, across
open land, far into December's
forest of leafless trees, out there,
in stillness, where the sound of wind
rises—that wildness again
that stripped the branches—
and singular how it's sensed,
so natural the seeming,
the metaphysical silence
ingathered there, just
as things have always been,
and he having spoken in praise
so often of what is wild
among wildflowers
and emanations of light,
where, in the nature of things,
peaks are sacred
where a day takes

what can't be banished—his words
borne from Tysmenytsia . . .
even upon his passing away,
a way.

PART III

TRANSIT

A day of light rain
on a path by the house . . .
I caught my fall on a stone
and held the pain in my palm,

an indwelling at the hub of touch,
its pulse an ache, as if to see,
yet a wound held apart.
It was bleeding.

With forearm and shoulder I shielded it,
as if it were some hurt animal
as I went for the bandage, a small barricade
against the thoroughfare,

and I remembered once,
when rain turned to sleet, houses along the road
entered evening, when
suddenly a lamp lit a window,

night's first room illumined,
how that warmed me, unprepared
as I was then for the enveloping cold.
I told myself, You'll not be lost

when the snow comes.

EMPIRES

> I hate fences, any kind of fence.
> —AI WEIWEI

Like a caravan camped
in snow falling from no country,
white tents and canopies
crowd Market Square.

Here two months of snow,
and "Are you French?"
a vendor says, in Ukrainian.
"Ni," I say, "Amerykans'kyy."

Gray light in the leafless poplars
and darkness gathering,
borderless, thick as flocks
of crows crossing in air . . .

In my room, the green tile stove
warms my hands. The shadow
cast from the amber pilot light
is a map on the wall.

The brass buckle slips
a notch further round my waist,
gone a little more
the heft from my land,

and CHINA stamped in gold dye
on the back tip of my belt . . .
shapes of frost, an atlas
on the windowpanes.

Chernivtsi

THE ERSTWHILE FORESTS

The match flame held above what was
first briar root, Mediterranean, then
artisan's block to carve a parabola
for a pipe to fit a palm—

                          light grows,
burning across the horizon line
I lower to chopped, cured leaves
and follow round the rim of the bowl,
as I breathe rapidly through the amber stem,
exhaling from a harvest of leaves,
large, dusty leaves casting shadows
once over red clay furrows in July,
leaves cut, bundled in a warehouse,
leaves blessed by the auctioneer
moving among them, calling out
a foreign language of peppered rhythms,
their flow of numbered sounds
rising through air now
as aromatic smoke, an apparition
bathed by breath. —

A flick of wrist kills light,
its gray tendril climbing long after
its tree was there.

OFF THE PATH

Down the slope from the rusted footbridge
a car passes under, I hear
the yelp and howl of stray dogs,
gravel shifting beneath my boots,
the clank of keys buried in my heavy clothes,
and, for a distance, the clatter
of a 19th century army, Blue or Gray,
intermontane and bivouacked—
low fires curling up from the camp.

I walk down, as in uniform,
toward the creek, a mile on before darkness.
Drops of rain pay their toll to me
and to the soaked terrain.
Mist gathers thick in the bare branches.
We sleep on our arms,
and it is said, "Let the dead
bury the dead." By this,
too many have been taken care of.

But resilience survives the worm-worked soil.
With grief at our heels,
grief at the elbows of forward observers,
only the mournful bugle
eases us, our stay warmed
by the steam of wet embers.
When the rain falls back, snow melts
in each footprint, each a wound
punched down to the red clay.

I cross the creek
and like smoke at a certain height,
the campaigns disappear.
A late breeze rallies
a tree of dead leaves,
a reassurance to spite the season.

THE SHRIMP TRAPPERS

Deep in the mountains,
two shrimp trappers carry
leaded nets across a meadow
in late November.

They spread the nets
over the frozen ground
and mark where they are—watermarks
whittled on the tall stakes.

Come December,
the first heavy snowfall,
the trappers return
in the thick gray of morning twilight.

They carry their wicker baskets
in the hull of a white bateau.
They lay the boat on the wind-combed surface
at the meadow's edge: they stand and stare.

At last, after the millenniums
of hibernation, this high tide. . . .
The shrimp have settled in russet arcs
in the bright expanse.

From their boat set down
among the shrimp beds
the trappers pull the lines,
and the rays of shadow lengthening

and the nets again, rising from the undulations.

QUESTION IN LAMPLIGHT

I have made my way up the mountain.
I have made my way through the house
of many rooms and found the tall stairs
dark at the top, no matter the daylight
above the trees—

              the first steps shining
in the electric glow from a single sconce.
Are these the stairs where at their height
a door, the last, opens to the summit?

Kyiv

AT ST. JOHN THE DIVINE, THINKING
OF MELVILLE

Past the tympanum's bronze doors
under the rose window,
as many times years ago,
on late afternoons, I hear
only my steps on the marble floor.

Under the height of granite
and all things still,
I sit on a folding chair
at the end of a Hundred and Twelfth
and Amsterdam, the end of an aisle

far from the altar—
no detail seen at the ceiling,
a perpetual dark—faint, stained glass
more luminous as I stare.

Out in the garden "the unstained
light of open day"—
                        cherry blossoms
shadowing crooked trunks
                             provide
for the bees, humming, just
here, off the sidewalk—late

sunlight at Morningside Heights.

FOUNDING CITIES

for my son Will

Eventually, where we are
will be found between a there
and a there, and here we are, two o'clock,
a Sunday afternoon in May,
sunlight on the maples along the Tiber
and breeze enough to make the leaves tremble,
to rock gently the branches between
the dark current and loud cars
and Vespas passing the Ponte Sisto.

That breeze now, in here, ruffles the tall drapes,
their delicate, flowered embroidery.
The pane is cracked nearly the height of the window,
likely a beer bottle smack, its leisurely line
like a trail or creek mapped through Stone Valley,
our home in Pennsylvania, its passage
natural as graffiti on the arched columns
next door at Via del Politeama, as on a wall
off Broad Street in Philadelphia—here and there,

winged seeds and dust through the air.

SANDS STREET

Gulls calling, soaring past towered pairs
of arches—granite mortared,
steel bolted—each a niche for sky . . .
eastbound, I cross Brooklyn Bridge.

At Sands Street under a tree
fat with buds, yellow hues at their tips,
ants journey the lengthening shadow of
shade between sidewalk squares.

Then back across the bridge,
where from this height a little terror
in the current of elation: in a sense
the liquid eye is architect of all there is.

At the Municipal Building's plaza across
from the Emigrant Industrial Savings Bank,
an ant, a bee, a butterfly forage at my table . . .
ever here the changing storefronts

from sacrificed forests . . . ever the wars we wage
against ourselves, yet minerals of the granite island
remain in its people, varied, elemental,
in veins spreading through strata,

and what's been saved, if only
in the mind's eye, that lasting place,
is a principle of the Buddha, as in Bamiyan
after his statues are blown apart.

APART

A shared domain, the instant absolute,
Piero's *Victory of Constantine over Maxentius*—
    dividing the scene, a horse stumbles

    from mire at the mouth of a river.
An ear toward pursuit, the rider,
    gripping the reins, stares beyond us—

    his future. Below the eyes
of Constantine's white horse,
    a village upriver at the horizon,

    a swan and her two cygnets,
their moment apart is reflected
    on a tree's shadow:

    gradations on a sky-blue of still water—
the river having flooded its banks,
    the flood from what must have been

    rain coming down like arrows.
The rider's isolate, blank terror
    through layers of light,

    his open gaze at the edge
of sorrow we recognize, despite the near
    blindness in which we live,

    and here a man, his sudden awareness:
duration is patience preserving
    presence through the ongoing, the violence.

THE RITUAL

I stood holding a rope end
at a barn the morning
my grandfather,
the county veterinarian,
made me one of the tribe.

We brought the colt down
gently by the galvanized tub
on the grass. Grandfather
shredded sheets, dropping strips
into a milky antiseptic.

As if to draw an arc, pencil
on paper, he drew the scalpel
over the scrotum. Blue-veined,
bloodless as a boiled egg,
a gray testicle was born.

Ball in hand, he cut the muscle.
All the while the horse was walleyed.
Staring, I pulled the rope end
tighter, hopeful that holding down
the horse was not dependent on me.

When the next testicle
was taken, I wanted to let go,
but we all held taut while Grandfather
stuffed wads of sheet into the cavity.
He stitched the loose skin.

He patted the horse.
We dropped our ropes.
In that way a horse will stand,
he stood, still at first
to gain his bearings.

Being tamed as he was,
he walked within
that mute circle of the ritual.
I was listening to rags
slopping the emptiness.

AT MEADOW'S EDGE

for Jen and Pat

Dawn of a clear day, song bursts after snowfalls,
breaths above yellow blossoms:
purple martins circle the meadow and creek, to cove
opening wide to the bay—each loop
deepening the familiarity of familiar terrain—

the tideline a point of return,
homecoming to a stand of birches,
their lavish shadows on the meadow,
each tree at standstill and free
as wanderers here through days, nights, seasons,

each branch by chance a harbor
for a martin to rest, as if adrift from winter's
gray days till now: white clouds
billowing across a blue sky, this long
instance of ardor and calm. —

Dawn holding night's place,
my shadow among all else here,
night an absence for a time, the moon,
orbit full, a moonstone sunk below the light
of our sun's perfect circle,

all the while the stars shift, it seems,
their places as we travel our great ellipse,
their depths changing by the hour
the slow montage of night,
countless their lights wavering . . .

with the dawn wingbeats of martins
in purple constellations—such equality shared

minutely through the infinite distance
in the welter, the vaster way of gods, races, nations:
stations along the way

in the loops of martins; and always,
suddenly, somewhere, an old man and woman
thrust up their arms at the violent death
of someone, as if at the next instant
gravity might cease to exist. —

Wind, rising and falling, strips
new leaves and the last autumn leaf.
Imagine a stray martin perched,
for a moment of freedom, on your shoulder,
an elsewhere. . . . Here, sometimes,

what we know we'll have forgotten
and, no longer knowing, discover
what we've never known, revealed
at the water's edge, as if to sustain
a juncture of place, a memory

to touch all else: a creek flowing down
its furrow over the cove's stones and shells,
the tide going out, small waves lapping stillness
under an arc of daylight—unfixed now,
moving on—not a breeze through leaves,

yet all is animate,

as if stones

might rise and circle together into flight.

PART IV

.

COVE

Something deep has stirred,
something still unconscious, yet rising
and you sense it, as if seen where you are,
and it travels with you, and you
not knowing you are home already,

and here with you the leafless oak
lives on for the moment, though it's only
an image, a tree in a stand of pine and birch
in a forest and a blue jay finding
its song mixed with complaint,

and you sensing some change,
remembering the evergreens . . .
feeling moreover a calm provision,
as on a good night, when calm
arrives in sleep—its images

from dream's gallery furthering
its fresh arrangement, you,
the outsider encompassed, discovering
moments, what is made by you,
the vision and echo in you,

their trees real as memory
as you stood listening . . .
and you seeing the colors here,
the lines upon planes: bare oak,
underbrush and birch and pine,

a blue sky, the luminous clouds
reminding you of a face or animal,
or one thing becoming another,
risen to recognition and you
imagining what is vast

within this close circumference:
a sea, its waves lengthening
their portions of light, and you with
your small jars of water and oil
to mix a potion for color

to make a place, a further origin
in time to come, where—with its song
intermittent now—the loud jay
flies past and will
return when conscience

and color are inseparable, equal
to what you sense, the loose
calculations drawn to the nth
degree, the bird a streak of light
and stillness upon the canvas,

a current of light moving
deep within the panorama
and you feeling close enough
to touch a ghost beyond
the parameters of the first seen

from what was always to be
suddenly here, the now from what
seemed endless, the never-before
horizon line, the new
orientation of where you are,

and having always been
on the way, the crow will find you:
like hard rain, the crow's *kahr*,
and yet tranquil as ash after rain,
the jay's soft *queedle-queedle, queedle,*

not the jay's hawk-like shrieks—
jeeah, jeeah—but singular
tranquility, a *queedle* entering
the numb shadow of violence, cry
to song, a blazing afternoon to dusk,

the song a reprieve, as though
there were a cage, its door, and tension
of the lock loosened, the click to sudden
passage, as if, branch to branch,
an ascent beyond the taloned hour,

and you alone in silence,
in the warmth of promise of
sunrise, even if in the chill of winter,
and you to be the mapmaker
for the new terrain of all you see

across the forest
at daybreak, a jay flying slowly
from tree to tree, this seen once—
your anticipation stirred—how such
a place is to feel such,

you, one of countless people
now who have felt such
upon seeing the common bird,
each sensation peerless in
the instant of awareness, this spell,

like pigment on a cave wall,
brushstroke in the firelight,
no matter the bleakness of days:
a family dressed in bison skin
is dancing motion's moment

in stillness—its equilibrium,
a symmetry with a small flock
of ocher birds ascending upon the wall
and one bird perched on a branch above
the packed earth of the cave—

their world born from water and earth
to sounds from a little flute made
from marrowbone—what was that song?—
and that bird transfigured from where,
unseen except for *this*,

a distillation in a natural shelter,
its domain the common region
of hostile landscapes, the bird,
its profile the image of interdiction,
an encompassing shape of survival

as on a cave wall, near Aleppo, painted shapes
saved from ancient caravans passing
to Baghdad, and from Hittites, Assyrians, Persians,
Alexander the Great, then Romans, Arabs, Crusaders,
the Mongols, Ottomans, Egyptians, the French,

then from the house of Assad
and the Russians and the long shadows from Iran
and the House of Saud—the days, nights, months,
these many years under siege—come the helicopters,
the jets, the barrel bombs, the poison gas,

missiles upon the Syrians, the sounds of velocities
closing in from above, the incoming, incoming,
incoming, incoming, and the detonations
and detonations . . . detonations, fire flaring
and clouds of dust from concrete rubble,

then the silence following
and trapped, the dead, the dying,
and the rush for life, and from the rubble
the infant and child, dust covered,
staring from the video of a mobile phone

into the eyes of someone
there to save them, then into
the beyond and back, and in
that silence a survivor feels
life surging back into the body,

and when that silence lasts a little longer,
trees are leveled for firewood, leaves stripped
and cooked, and if there is a place
in mind within the terror, if just this,
for the jay's shriek, then jay, its mate,

and if a longer silence, the song,
if only an instant of promise in the hollow
of fear—our primal origin:
small fire in a cave—such is light
in a basement shelter

and ancient the charcoal lines
for birds in a tree on a cave wall,
and a child draws a jay among
new leaves of an oak, knowing
oaks lie broken in the street,

there an acorn among the ruins for a crow
in the poisoned air and still a jay will flutter through
a broken wall and perch in a garden bush, turn
its head up quickly from side to side
and chant its Eurasian song,

piyeh . . . piyeh, a descending mew, as if
from a dense forest—quietude of a natural citadel—
as if from wisdom, a song for our species
capable of such destruction, with memory now
of an olive grove at the wind-stilled hour

of sunset, the song a calm hand
upon a shoulder wanting ever "Just
to *be* safe," knowing well the ancestral truth,
"When elephants fight, it is the grass
that suffers," then night, soon to be a place

of stillness—of feather,
fingertip, fur, the chosen stick or bone,
a ballpoint pen, a brush to slow the heart,
to breathe deeply to imagine
what might be—to enfold

the living in light below
the terror . . . gods ever at war
in a stunned city, nightmares
invading the day and the bird flies on,
and you now near sunrise,

the tide turning out
quietly from the cove—
from night's downpour and thunder,
from thick fog
at first light clearing—

the whitecaps gone, waves easing out
under a driftwood oak—the untold stones
and life to be revealed in tidepools
in the sun—a province
part of and apart from past,

the sea a solvent of what was,
yet your abiding breath
a presence, what you must feel,
a separation in suspension,
illumination taken deep

into perspective, to make from this place
our return to the living
from carbon of ash in the pigment,
a sky made from earth,
the observance a transfiguration

from light by light touch,
mind conjuring what we see
in measured space, though the straight line
and curve be imperfect,
in touch with our single pulse,

as figures on the rock wall,
life from life, a dance close as kin, home
in currents of light, the inexhaustible
in a pause for life,
when so much has been taken by time,

and the first bird
at sunup sings, with gull and crow
foraging among stones,
and the jay's blue radiance
in an angle of light

on a branch, leaf buds
greening, the remembrance already
of how it is, yet never quite like before,
the presence of stillness,
then wind off the cove,

the shadows cast—
infinite curvatures, a solidity
in the ether of time, bird and tree,
first brushstroke to canvas
and lapis now to paint the jay.